the Green Song

by

DORIS TROUTMAN PLENN

illustrations by BRAD TEARE

HARCOURT BRACE & COMPANY

Orlando Atlanta Austin Boston San Francisco Chicago Dallas New York
Toronto London

Illustrations by Brad Teare
Illustrations copyright © 1994 by Harcourt Brace & Company

This edition is published by special arrangement with Doris Troutman Plenn.

Grateful acknowledgment is made to Doris Troutman Plenn for permission to
reprint *The Green Song* by Doris Troutman Plenn. Text copyright 1954 by
Doris T. Plenn.

Printed in the United States of America

ISBN 0-15-302197-7

   4 5 6 7 8 9 10   011   97 96 95

For my niece
Armande Elisa Troutman
on the occasion of her birth

Part One

There is a very little people who live on the Island of Puerto Rico, a summer land, where the weather is always warm. They look like tree frogs, but they are called coquis. They live in green plants and many of them prefer this color to all others. These coquis like everything to be green. Things that are not green, they believe, are not as good as things that are green.

In the evening, just after the sun has gone down, all of them come out on the porches of their houses, which are built in the plants, and start to work. They feel it right in their bones when it is time to start and so they are never late. They never allow anything to keep them from working and they call what they do the Green Work. They believe it is the most important work in the whole world and they do it very well. The work is singing. One coqui will begin to sing and then another will join in. "Coqui, coqui," they sing. After this, many others join in and a few stop for a while. Then those who stopped first start again and the others rest. Then they all sing together and after a while some stop. Then others begin again. They do this for a long time every evening and night. It makes a loud and lovely song and they think the whole world listens.

It is called, of course, the Green Song. The coquis believe that this song holds everything together. They believe that the Green Song holds the stars in place and makes the moon shine. They think that if they did not sing the Green Song every evening, the stars would fall down and everything would be upset. Because they sing it the moon shines, or the clouds come out; and, when the night is over, the sun is able to come up in its place. It is the Green Song that makes a place in the sky for the sun. The coquis believe that the order in the skies is made by their Green Work which they do by singing the Green Song all together. Others do not believe this, but the coquis say it is the truth.

Now the coquis are a very small people, but the smallest of all was Pepe Coqui. Every day people, who were much bigger and always spoke of themselves as People with a capital P, came to work in the sugar cane field which grew around the house where Pepe lived. He felt rather sorry for them because they did not live in among the sugar cane stalks where it was all green. He once told them so, frankly, but they only laughed. One of them, whose name was Juan, took Pepe in his hand and spoke to him in a kind voice.

"Little brother, there are many colors in the world. Green is only one of them."

Pepe was astonished. "What a strange way to think!" he said.

When he was not busy with the Green Work, Pepe talked to the People. Every day they told him about a city far off called New York.

"My cousin went to live there," Juan told Pepe, "and he writes letters to me about it."

The sister of another and the uncle of still another one had gone there. Most of the People, it turned out, had friends or relatives in New York. It was a city of wonders, they told Pepe. And again Pepe was astonished. "I thought the sugar cane field was the most wonderful place," he said.

"Oh, the sugar cane field is fine," Juan said, "but it is not at all like New York. New York is *different*."

Another of the People, whose name was Rafael, bent down and explained carefully to Pepe:

"They say New York is *bigger*."

"And they say it is *better*," Juan added.

Pepe thought for a moment. "It must be a very green place," he told them, and they laughed.

Juan sat down beside Pepe and said, "Friend, I will tell you the truth. You cannot see clearly as yet. Everything is all green to you because you have lived in a sugar cane field all your life. You have not seen the world."

Pepe frowned. "Where is the world?"

"The world is here—"

"Well, then," Pepe smiled. "I have seen it."

"Ah, but the world is also away from here. New York is the place to see the world."

"Why?" asked Pepe.

"Because all the world comes to New York."

"All the world comes to New York to see the world? Are you sure you understand this matter?"

"Friend, you ask too many questions."

"Well, how am I to find out?"

"If you saw the world you would not ask so many questions," Juan said.

"Why not?"

"Because you would see with your own eyes and there would be no need to ask." Juan and Rafael wanted to go back to their work, so they turned away.

Pepe thought for a long time. "I would like to see the world," he told them in his loudest voice just as they were starting to work again. "Yes, indeed, I would."

"Very well," Rafael said. "Go and see it."

"I think I will go."

"Well, go," he was told.

"I would like to go to New York."

"Go, then," said Juan. "Go somewhere."

At that moment Pepe felt it in his bones that it was time to start the Green Work, so he began to sing. All the people left the sugar cane field when

Pepe started to sing because they knew it was time to go home. Pepe turned his face up to the sky and the Green Song hopped from his throat in round, loud notes. All the other coquis, near and far, worked with him and soon Pepe felt that the notes were piling up in the sky, one on top of the other, like steps. They reached farther and farther upward until they came to the top, where they pushed one star in place, pulled out another one, polished a few to make them shine more brightly, and separated several which were just a little crowded. Then, at the right moment, the moon— whose place for the night had been well dusted by the notes of the Green Song—sailed out and shone down. Pepe felt that the Green Work was going well, and that made him happy.

When everything was in order in the sky for the night and a place had been made for the sun to come up the next morning, Pepe sat down on his porch and rested. Soon a friend of his, Coco Coqui, came by to see him. They sat in the moonlight on the porch and talked.

"Coco, I think I will go to New York."

"You do?" asked Coco. "Where is that?"

"Oh, it's in the world."

"It is? Where is that?"

"It's—well, it's everywhere."

"It is? Where is everywhere?"

"Coco, excuse me, but it seems to me that you say things over and over."

"I do? How is that?"

"I like you very much, Coco, but sometimes you ask too many questions."

"I do? What are they?"

"Why, they are the things you ask when you raise your voice at the end of saying something."

"I do *that*?"

"Yes."

"Don't all coquis do that?"

"As I was telling you, Coco, I think I will go and see New York. It is a very big place."

"It is? How big?"

"But right now, Coco, I am going to bed. Good night."

"You are? Good night."

The next morning, when the People came to work in the sugar cane field, Pepe was waiting for them. He hopped up to Juan and asked, "How do I get there?"

"Where, Pepe?"

"To New York, of course. I want to visit the world."

"Well, it's a long way off. You must cross the water."

"The water? You mean it will be raining?"

"No, little brother, I mean the ocean. It is a great deal of water with fishes in it. And waves."

"Ocean and fishes and waves. These are new words," Pepe said.

"They are old words," said Juan. "They are just new to you."

"Well, then, they are new words."

"Oh," cried Rafael. "What shall we tell him? He knows nothing of the blue waves and the red and golden and purple fishes!"

"What is blue and red and golden and purple?" Pepe asked Juan and Rafael.

"Yes, truly," Juan said, "the poor little one lives in the dark. It is as though he were blind, almost. Now listen, Pepe. You will see for yourself. You will ride on one of the airplanes. They go over the ocean. They fly."

"They do? How do they do it?"

"Inside of themselves they have a great motor. It hums and then it sings. And after that it makes things move."

"Why, just like me!" Pepe smiled.

Juan and Rafael shook their heads. They did not believe that the Green Song kept order in the sky, but they could not tell this to Pepe because he would not have believed *them*. "Well, not exactly," Rafael told him. "It sings another song."

Pepe was shocked. "Of course! Naturally it cannot sing the Green Song! I will go flying with the airplane to New York. Where will I find it?"

"At the airport. But first you must buy a ticket."

"Where will I buy it?"

"A man will be waiting behind a little window at the airport. You buy the ticket from him. And then you give it to another man on the airplane."

"Why can't the man in the airport give it to the other man?"

"Because," said Juan, "it is required for everybody to get it from one and give it to the other."

Pepe sighed. "The world is a strange place, isn't it?"

"Ah, but I would like to know more about it," Juan said.

"You would? I will go now and visit it. When I come back I will tell you all about it."

"You will be a bigger person for having seen it," said Rafael.

"I will? Will I grow?"

"It is a way of speaking, little brother. You will grow inside," Juan explained.

"But if I grow inside, won't I push myself out and grow on the outside, too?"

"Perhaps," said Juan. "But be very careful, my friend. Watch yourself."

"How can I watch *myself* if I am going to look at the world?"

"It is a way of speaking," Juan sighed. "We will miss you."

"Of course," Pepe agreed. "Good-by."

Then he looked around for his friend Coco. "Now I am starting out on my visit to the world," he told him.

"You are really going, Pepe? When will you come back?" There were tears in Coco's eyes.

"When my visit is over, naturally. Good-by, Coco."

"Pepe, good-by." Sadly Coco waved to Pepe and watched him go down the road.

Part Two

But Pepe was happy. He waved back once to Coco, then set off briskly for the airport. He traveled nearly all day, going through the green grass along the edges of the roads, and asking the way now and then from fellow coquis whom he met. By and by he came to the airport. He found the little window where a man was selling tickets. Suitcases and boxes were piled up like steps on one side of it and Pepe climbed and hopped up over these until he reached the counter in front of the window. "I want to buy a ticket. I am going to New York," he said.

"Get in line," said the Ticket Seller.

"Where is that?" Pepe asked.

"Get behind the last person waiting there," and the Ticket Seller pointed out the place for Pepe.

Pepe hopped to the place and waited. Soon the person ahead of him stepped forward a little way, and so did Pepe. "I am going to New York," Pepe told him. But the person said nothing. He just stood there in line.

"Perhaps he didn't hear me," Pepe thought and he shouted louder. This time the person turned but then, after looking around a second, he turned back.

"I am down here!" Pepe yelled.

The person looked down, and sure enough, he saw Pepe. "Why, it's a coqui!" he exclaimed.

"Naturally, I'm a coqui," Pepe said proudly. "I am going to New York."

"Don't tell me that!" the person said. "Don't tell me that coquis are leaving the Island and going to New York!"

"Not the coquis. Only me. I'm Pepe Coqui. Only I am going."

The person seemed to feel better. "Oh, then it's all right. We cannot do without our coquis."

"Of course not," Pepe agreed.

"Are you looking for work?" the person asked politely.

"*Looking* for work? I have my own work. It is the Green Work, of course."

"And you can do it anywhere?"

"Naturally. I am a coqui." Pepe drew himself up to his tallest height.

"How lucky you are! Now I am going to New York to look for work." At that moment the Ticket Seller called and the person left Pepe.

And then, next, it was Pepe's turn. He hopped up on the counter. "Now just what *is* a ticket?" he asked the man.

The Ticket Seller pushed his spectacles up on

his forehead and looked at Pepe carefully. "A ticket," he said, "is a piece of paper that shows you have bought a seat on the plane."

"What can I do with the seat after I buy it?"

"You can sit on it."

"Oh, you mean a chair!" Pepe said. "How big is this chair?"

"It's a seat, and it's that big." The Ticket Seller pointed to a chair in the office where he stood.

"Well, that," said Pepe, "is a chair. Are you sure you understand about these matters?"

"Of course I understand! A chair can be a seat!"

"I am not sure that you do. For instance, anyone could see that that chair is too big for me."

"Who cares?" The Ticket Seller began to shout.

Pepe was astonished. "Why, I do! And what if I fell off? And then, too, there is the matter of the cost."

"The cost is the same for every seat."

"Even if one only sat on a corner of it?"

"Nobody sits on a corner of it! A seat is for one person! It fits one person!"

"It doesn't fit me. Look!"

Pepe hopped down from the counter and sat on the seat inside the office. The ticket man had to put his spectacles back on to see him because he was so small and the chair was so big. The ticket man scratched his head. "How could we strap you in it?" he asked.

"Strap me?"

"Everyone must have a strap around him to hold him safely when the plane flies off the ground."

"In that case, I most certainly require a seat my size," Pepe told him with dignity.

"Just a minute," the Ticket Seller said. "You wait here and I will come back." He went out of his office holding his head in his hands. He went to the office of his chief, and threw himself into a chair.

"I have a coqui in my office," he told the chief.

"Oh, that's all right," the chief answered. "They don't bite, you know. Or sting, or anything ugly like that."

"But this one wants to buy a ticket to New York."

The chief's eyes brightened. "Well, sell him one."

"He won't buy a regular one. He says the seat is too big. And there is something to what he says. The seat looks much bigger when he sits on it."

"Hmmmmm," said the chief. "I'd better look into this. This is the first time a coqui has asked for a ticket. We'd better take good care of him. He is the first, but he may not be the last." The chief laughed and patted the Ticket Seller on the back cheerfully.

The two went back to the Ticket Seller's office where Pepe was waiting. He was still sitting in the middle of the big seat. "How do you do, sir?" the chief greeted him.

"Very well, I thank you," Pepe replied. "Except in the matter of a seat to go on my visit to the world."

"Hmmm," said the chief. "It is a little roomy, isn't it? And you are going to visit the world, you say?"

"Oh, yes."

"You want a round-the-world ticket, I suppose?"

"No, I want a New York ticket."

"No doubt he will go in stages," the chief whispered to the Ticket Seller. "New York first, you know. Good service may persuade him to travel farther with our company." Then aloud he said, "Now let's see what we can do about the proper seat for you. Hmmmmm. I will call *my* chief."

The chief called his chief, and this chief called the first vice-president, who called two more vice-presidents who decided it was a matter for the Traffic Manager. The Traffic Manager thought it should be taken care of by the captain and officers of the plane. They talked a while and then the engineer said, "I think I will be able to fix it. Yes, indeed. How big is he?"

"He's not very big," the Ticket Seller said. "About this big." He measured a space in the air with his hands.

"Oh, no," said his chief. "He's *this* big." And he, too, measured the air with his hands.

"I will have to measure him myself," said the engineer. He took a ruler and went in where Pepe was still waiting. "It is getting rather late," Pepe said.

"Yes, indeed," the engineer replied. "Would you be good enough to sit on this ruler, please?"

"Why?"

"To see what your size is."

"I am the smallest of the coquis."

"But I must know your size exactly. I am the engineer."

By now Pepe was expecting things to be strange, so, although no one had ever before asked him to sit on a ruler, he hopped over and tried to sit on this one. It was not an easy thing to do because the ruler was made of shiny wood and was not only hard but slippery as well. Pepe slid down from it a few times, but finally he got a good grip on it with his feet and sat down. The engineer was standing behind him. "Is this the way?" Pepe called over his shoulder.

"Yes, indeed," the engineer said. He looked down at Pepe on the ruler. "Well, now, let me see. It seems that you are almost an inch in size."

"I am?" Pepe was pleased. "That's a very fine size, I suppose?"

"Oh, yes, indeed. I think that now we can fix a seat that will be just right."

"Well, I hope so. I am going to cross the water that has the new words in it."

"What new words?"

"Well, I cannot remember them now, but when I see them I will know. That's why I'm going to visit the world."

"Excuse me," said the engineer and ran out

17

of the office.

The Ticket Seller came back. "The engineer seems to be in a hurry," he said.

"He's hurrying to fix my seat. I told him it was getting late," Pepe informed him.

"Well, now that everything is settled, please make yourself comfortable. Your seat will be ready for the next plane, and they are having a talk about the price of your ticket."

"Will the price be according to size?" Pepe asked him.

"Well, yes."

"In that case," Pepe told him, "the price will be almost an inch."

"Almost an inch of what?"

"That is my size. I am almost an inch. I sat on the ruler."

"We don't sell tickets like that!"

"Like what?"

"By the inch!" the Ticket Seller shouted.

"You said it was according to size—"

"It is—but not like that! Money doesn't come by inches!"

"Well, you said the ticket would be by size, and as I told you, *that*," Pepe said firmly, "is almost an inch. Then I will measure the money to that."

Once again the Ticket Seller ran out of his office holding his head in his hands. He went into the room where the two chiefs and the three vice-presidents were holding their meeting. They looked at him, surprised.

"There is no reason for any of you to think about this problem any longer," he told them. "He"— and the Ticket Seller pointed to his office—"has got it all settled."

"Why, that's fine," said the first vice-president.

"Just a minute. Who has got it all settled?" asked the second one, who had been dozing.

"The coqui! The one in my office! The ticket is to be according to size—his size—which, he says over and over, is almost an inch!"

"Be calm," said the third vice-president. "We must face this bravely."

"Hmmmm," said the Ticket Seller's chief, "this is a new idea."

"And I don't think much of it," the second vice-president added.

"It may be the right answer, and again it may not be," said the first vice-president. "Let's go in and talk to him."

When they came into the office Pepe greeted them politely. "What can I do for you?" he asked.

"Well, it's about this ticket," the first vice-president began.

"Didn't the Ticket Seller explain to you?" Pepe asked in surprise.

"Yes, but how, exactly, would it work?"

"That is what *I* would like to know," said Pepe. "Here is the ruler. Now you measure a ticket, almost an inch size, you know."

The men nodded to the Ticket Seller. His

hands trembled as he put the ticket on the ruler. "I never thought I would be doing anything like this," he said. "Here, this is almost an inch."

"Well, cut that off," Pepe explained patiently.

The Ticket Seller cut off the ticket and gave it to Pepe. Pepe held up a dollar bill. He measured the bill to the ticket. "Almost an inch is not quite a quarter of a dollar," he said in a pleasant voice.

The Ticket Seller jumped. "It is not enough money!"

"It's according to size," Pepe told them all.

"I think," said the first vice-president, "we had better let it go for the moment. Later, we can have many talks and decide about the regular price of coqui tickets."

The others thought the first vice-president's words were very wise. They nodded to each other, breathed a sigh of relief, and the Ticket Seller gave the ticket to Pepe. Pepe gave him the money. Then each of the men bowed to Pepe. "We hope you have a pleasant trip," they said, one by one, as they left.

"I hope so, too," Pepe answered.

In the plane the carpenters worked on Pepe's seat. They put it on one side of the wall, near a window. Then they made a safety belt and put it around the seat. When it was all finished, the engineer went to the ticket office to tell Pepe that his plane was ready to go.

But just as he started to tell him, Pepe felt it in his bones that the sun had gone down some time ago and that it was time to begin the Green Work. So he raised his head and lifted his voice in the Green Song. The engineer tried to break into the singing, but Pepe frowned at him and continued. The Green Song is not to be interrupted. Outside the ticket office Pepe could hear the other coquis singing; one here, one there, until at last he heard them all join in together, starting and stopping at the right places.

"Coqui, coqui," they sang.

Pepe felt very good inside. He knew that the stars were coming out on time and that the moon, well dusted and polished by the notes of the Green Song, was getting ready to shine. "Coqui, coqui," sang all the coquis.

The engineer tried to get the Ticket Seller to help him stop Pepe's singing so that he could be told about the seat on the plane, but the Ticket Seller only put his hands to his ears and shook his head from side to side. The engineer tried to call the chiefs and vice-presidents but they said they preferred not to come back again. The Traffic Manager came, but Pepe frowned at him and went on with the Green Song.

Soon, People standing outside the ticket window put their heads through it and said to one another, "They've got a coqui in there."

A man said, "What are you doing to the coqui? Why is he calling so loudly for help?"

The Traffic Manager ran out of the office and so the Ticket Seller had to answer. "We aren't doing anything to him!" the Ticket Seller said.

"Then why is he crying like that?"

"He's just crying!"

"Why?" a lady asked.

"Who knows?" the Ticket Seller answered through the window. "He's trying to make us deaf!"

"Tch! tch! A little thing like that?"

A very strong man pushed his way to the window. "Aren't you ashamed to treat a small creature like that?" he asked.

Many other People came crowding around the ticket window and called out:

"Don't hurt our coquis!"

"We don't want our little coquis harmed!"

"I tell you nobody's harming him!" shouted the Ticket Seller.

"Then why don't you sell tickets and leave him alone?"

"Good idea," the engineer told the Ticket Seller. "Just go on with your work as though nothing was happening. We always do that when anything goes wrong with a plane. Yes, indeed."

"How can I work with that noise in my ears?" the Ticket Seller pointed to Pepe.

But the crowd outside was becoming more troublesome. Voices rose louder and louder.

"The coqui is waiting for his seat on the plane. He wants to go to New York," the Ticket Seller said loudly.

"Well, why don't you let him go?" the strong man asked.

"I'm not keeping him! His plane is ready to go and he sits there yelling!"

"Coquis don't yell," an elderly lady said indignantly. "*Such* language!"

"Look," the strong man began, "why don't you just leave him alone?"

"Who's bothering him? His plane will leave without him and it's the only one that has a seat his size!"

"Hold the plane!" "Send up another one!" "You've got lots of planes!" People in the crowd shouted out.

"I'll go tell them to warm up another plane," the engineer told the crowd. "We will keep his waiting a little longer. Oh, indeed, yes." Then he ran off.

"I should think so!" a lady said. "Hurrying a little thing like that until he's almost out of his wits!"

"With all your planes you certainly should be able to wait just a few minutes until a small coqui gets through crying! For all you know he may be heartbroken!" another lady spoke up.

"He's not crying! There's nothing wrong with his heart!" the Ticket Seller yelled.

"Well, he's scared, then. I'd not go around scaring little creatures if I were you, young man," the first lady said.

"Pick on somebody your size," the strong man spoke up loudly.

Suddenly Pepe stopped for a moment. It was

his turn to rest. "I am not crying. I am not scared. I am singing," he told everyone.

"Oh, the lovely creature! The darling!" all the ladies cried.

The Ticket Seller rushed over to Pepe. He wanted to hug him, but he was afraid the crowd would not understand. He patted Pepe's head and called out, "Did you hear? Now will you believe me?"

"Please," Pepe told him, "not so loud." And he began the Green Song again.

"You'd do well to attend to your work, young fellow, and leave coquis alone after this," the strong man said firmly.

The Ticket Seller stuffed his ears with cotton and began selling tickets. The People who wanted to buy tickets got in line, and the others went back to their seats in the waiting room. The ones who came to his window were not very friendly; they looked in at Pepe, singing away, and then glared at the Ticket Seller. He pulled an eyeshade down over his forehead and did not look up at anyone. He would say, "Where to?" and when he was told he would write out the ticket. In this way several hours passed.

Then, as suddenly as he had begun, Pepe stopped singing. He put his head on one side and listened. He heard the other coquis stop one by one. Everything was safe in the skies for the night and he felt contented. He hopped up on the counter where the Ticket Seller was writing out tickets. "Well, I'm ready," he said.

"Oh," cried the Ticket Seller when he saw Pepe before him. "You've stopped!" He took the cotton out of his ears.

"The Green Song is over for tonight. I will go now."

"You will? Honestly? You're sure?"

"Of course. Where is the plane?"

"That way," the Ticket Seller pointed. "Out that door. Can I help you go?"

"Thank you, no. I can help myself."

"You sure can!" The Ticket Seller fell back in his chair. He was very tired.

"Good-by," Pepe said as he left.

Part Three

*P*epe went through a big gate and hopped up the steps into the plane. All the other passengers were already seated and the motor was humming.

"Here is your seat, sir," the stewardess said to Pepe. He saw his seat near the window. It had a pillow on it. "I hope you will be comfortable, sir."

Pepe hopped up and sat down. "You do?" he asked.

"Yes, sir. Adjust your belt, please."

"Do what to my belt?"

"Tighten it. We are taking off."

"Tighten it, or take it off—which do you mean?"

"Excuse me, sir," said the stewardess. She leaned over and quickly bound the safety belt around Pepe.

"It's tight," he told her.

"It's supposed to be tight," she answered.

"My belt is tight," Pepe announced loudly to his neighbor.

"So is mine," the neighbor replied.

"I feel a little stuffed," Pepe told the stewardess.

"You can unbuckle it as soon as we get aloft."

"As soon as we get where?" Pepe asked.

"As soon as we get up in the air. The plane is still climbing."

"It is? I am climbing with it. I am going on a visit to the world."

"Would you like a drink of water?" the stewardess asked.

"Will it be the great water and have the new words in it?"

"How silly. It will be a paper cup and have water in it."

"In that case I don't believe I care for it," said Pepe.

"I will take your ticket now," the stewardess told him.

Pepe gave her the ticket. "It is almost an inch," he said with a dignified air.

She looked at him. "How can a ticket be almost an inch?"

"Because I am."

"A ticket has nothing to do with a person's size."

"Well," said Pepe, "you measure it and we will see." Then he turned and looked out the window.

He was up among the stars. They were very close to him. They blinked at him as the plane sailed by to show that they were his friends. "Hello, stars!" he called out.

The stewardess came back quickly. "You mustn't talk to the stars," she said in a low voice.

"I mustn't?"

"No. It's late and the passengers are trying to sleep." Then she went away.

"Are you trying to sleep?" Pepe asked his neighbor.

"Not very hard," the neighbor smiled.

"She said I mustn't talk to the stars," Pepe whispered.

"Many People say that. Don't pay too much attention to them," the neighbor whispered back.

"Why do they say it?"

The neighbor shook his head. "I don't know. I've been trying to figure it out for a long time. It's a mystery."

"It is? I've never talked to the stars before, but I've sung to them since I was born."

"So have I."

"You have? I am Pepe. Who are you?"

"I'm Alberto. I'm happy to know you."

"I am a coqui. I sing the Green Song."

"Yes, I know. I am a poet."

"You are? Does that mean one of the People who sings to the stars?"

"In a way of speaking, yes."

Pepe felt glad. "I am learning all the new words. I came on a visit to the world to learn them, and now I am doing it."

"It's a good thing to do. I try to do that, too."

"Do you know about the new words down in the big water?"

"I don't believe I do."

Pepe stared out the window. "It's so dark

down there. I cannot see the words."

"On my trip back to the Island I will go in the daytime and look for you. I will try to find the new words in the water when the sun is shining, and if I do I will tell them to you," the poet said.

"You will?" Pepe explained. "I will go back by day, too, and if I find them I will tell you."

"Thank you for telling me they were down there." Alberto smiled happily. "This is the way it has always been. Coquis have been helpful to poets since our Island was an island."

Pepe was astonished. "I never knew that!"

"Oh, yes. It goes back years and years. We— well, we understand each other."

"Oh, we do!"

The stewardess came with a little light and shone it on their faces. "Gentlemen," she said firmly, "your whispering is disturbing the other passengers. I must ask you to allow them to sleep." Then she went away.

"I don't think I care for her at all," Pepe whispered.

"She must be like that, Pepe. It is her work."

"It is?"

Alberto nodded and shrugged his shoulders. Then he and Pepe both sighed.

"Good night, Alberto," said Pepe.

"Good night," Alberto answered.

When they awoke it was morning. The stewardess came and said, "Good morning." She gave them coffee and rolls to eat.

Soon the motor stopped roaring and became quieter and quieter until at last it was still. The plane had landed.

"Is New York out there all around us?" Pepe asked.

"No. We must take a bus into New York. Why don't you get up on my shoulder and I'll give you a lift?"

"You will? I would like to go with you, Alberto." Pepe hopped from his seat up to Alberto's shoulder.

"Think you will be all right?" Alberto asked.

"Yes. I'll hold on to your collar."

Alberto got up and walked toward the door of the plane. Suddenly he stopped. Passengers were behind and in front of him. The one nearest him in back said, "Go forward, please." But Alberto didn't move.

"Isn't this the right place for us to get off after all, Alberto?" Pepe asked.

"Yes, but—" Alberto was looking all around him. The People behind began shoving a little to make him go forward. Suddenly Alberto stepped out of the aisle and sat down again on a seat. The other People went on by and out the door.

"Pepe," he said, "there is something I must tell you."

"You must? Shall I get down from your shoulder?"

"No, just stay where you are. I can tell you like this. Right outside the door, Pepe, there is a new word."

"There is?"

"It's a falling kind of a word. It's white."

"What is white?"

"White is the color of the new word. And it is cold, Pepe. Do you remember how it feels sometimes in the winter—after a long rain?"

"I shiver. Sometimes I shake. Then I go into my house."

"That is being chilly. Cold is like that except much, much more. The new word is *snow*. It falls out of the sky, and it is white and cold. Look out the window, Pepe."

Pepe did. Snow was blowing everywhere. There was nothing else to see but snow. "It is not green," said Pepe. "It is the color of shivering and shaking." He trembled and moved closer to Alberto's collar.

"Did you bring an overcoat, Pepe?"

"An overcoat?"

"A coat to put on to keep you warm."

"No."

"Well, let me see what I have." Alberto went through all his pockets. He took out a handkerchief and started to wrap it around Pepe. "No," he said, "it is not warm enough. Also, it is too big." Then he went through his pockets again and found a penwiper. "Now this is what I use to keep my pens clean. It has a spot of ink on it, but it is a very little spot. The important thing is that it is made of wool and will be warm."

"Yes," Pepe agreed. Alberto wrapped it around him.

"It looks fine," Alberto said. "Here, just let me fold back a collar for you and pin it all together. Now we can go. The snow is pretty, Pepe, if one is warm."

"It is?"

"You can look at it better when we get outside."

They started to walk to the door. At that moment the stewardess came into the plane with two big men. She pointed to Alberto. "There he is. He's the one you were asking about."

"Oh, no," said Alberto softly.

"He is not the one!" Pepe shouted. Then into Alberto's ear he added, "The one what, Alberto?" But Alberto only shook his head.

"What's that?" one of the big men asked. "I heard a funny sound. Did you?"

"Yes, I did. But come on. We've got to get him down to the Hall. They're waiting for him."

The big men stood on either side of Alberto. "The City's glad to see you. Let's go now," one of them said.

When they left the plane, the two big men walked very fast across the airfield. "Where are we going, Alberto?" cried Pepe. But again Alberto only shook his head, dismally. They came to a large automobile and Alberto and Pepe got into the back seat. The two men sat in the front and drove the car away through the thick falling snow. Pepe clung to Alberto's collar and whispered in his ear, "I'll stay with you."

"Oh, Pepe, thank you!" Alberto said gratefully. They were silent for a little while.

"Is this the bus?" Pepe asked.

"No, it's a car," Alberto answered. He was slumped down in the seat. The car roared through the streets, going straight to the heart of the city.

Pepe shivered in his new overcoat. "The world is not green," he said.

"Are you cold, Pepe?"

"No. It's another kind of shivering. I don't know what it is."

"I do," Alberto told him. "It's because you feel that I am troubled. And you feel that we are together."

"It is a new feeling. What is it, Alberto? What is going to happen?"

But Alberto sank even lower in his seat. "For a little while, because I was talking to you, I forgot all about it. I can't talk about it."

"Then look at the snow, Alberto. It falls down, but it builds up hills and valleys on the ground."

Alberto looked out of the window. "Yes. The snow makes the world new again. It fills up all the empty places."

"It does?"

"The world has many places that we never knew were empty until we see them filled with snow. Look now, Pepe, we are in New York."

Suddenly there were more People around them than Pepe had ever seen. The car stopped and one of the men opened the door. "Here you are," he said. "Right this way." He took Alberto's arm and led him through all the People. Pepe held on tightly. They walked up many wooden steps and came to a wide place. There were only a few People here. Pepe looked around and saw that the great crowd of People was now below them. They were all looking up at the platform on which he was standing with Alberto. A man, who had been talking to the People below, came toward them. "Here he is, Your Honor," said the big man, leading Alberto forward. The new man now took Alberto's arm and began walking him to the front toward the People.

"You're just in time," he said. "We are ready for you. Stand right here beside me. I am the Mayor. I'm delighted to know you."

"I am happy to know you," Alberto said, bowing gracefully.

The Mayor turned and began talking to the People below. "And now," he said, "on this day which has been set aside and called The Day of the Island, when we meet to celebrate the deeds of those of the Island's People who have come to live among us, on this day it gives me the greatest joy to tell you that the most distinguished Islander of them all, the Islander whose poems and songs are known the world over—"

"Pepe," Alberto whispered, "this is good. But I feel awful."

"Is he talking about *you*, Alberto?"

Alberto tried to answer but he choked. So he just nodded "Yes."

Pepe looked down and saw, beyond the whirling snow, hundreds and hundreds of faces that were like the faces of the People he knew on the Island. The Mayor talked on.

"What does he want you to do, Alberto?"

"My throat won't work, Pepe," Alberto whispered.

"Does he want you to sing to the People?"

"In a manner of speaking, yes."

"Your throat must work to sing."

"You understand so well, Pepe. I always choke at times like this."

"Perhaps I could sing for you."

"Oh, Pepe! Would you? But it's not your time to sing! It's not evening, and it's cold! Do you think it might be wrong for you to try?"

"I don't think so. Of course I could only do a little piece of the Green Song, not the real thing, you know. Which side shall I sing to?"

"Straight out front. Right into that little machine the Mayor is talking into. It is a microphone."

"It is?"

They heard the Mayor's voice: "Here he is! The poet whose songs are like a call from the Island itself! The man whose name the civilized world honors!" The Mayor turned to Alberto and whispered, "What's the name?"

"Go ahead, Pepe," Alberto said, with a choke in his voice.

Pepe hopped down on the table and opened his mouth. Snow fell in it. "Coqui, coqui," he sang. But he had swallowed the snow and his notes went down his throat with it. The only sound Pepe made was a strange chirp.

"Oh, Pepe! Be careful!" Alberto cried.

"My word!" said the Mayor. "A cricket!"

Pepe drew himself up proudly. "I am a coqui!" he announced in a strong voice which went straight into the microphone. When he said it there was a great roar from the People below.

"A coqui!" they shouted.

"A coqui in New York!"

"Long live the coquis!"

They waved their handkerchiefs and laughed and clapped.

"Right here in all this snow—a cricket!" the Mayor said, not understanding Pepe or the People's words. "They seem to like him," he added, speaking to a man standing by him.

The man shook his head gloomily, as though to say that no one ought to expect him to believe such things happened.

"Chirp some more, little cricket," the Mayor told Pepe kindly.

Pepe opened his mouth again and the snow fell in, but this time he swallowed it before his notes leaped out. "Coqui, coqui," he sang. Then

he swallowed more snow and began again, singing part of the Green Song clearly and in tune. The People below were enchanted. They laughed and shouted and cried with joy.

But no coquis answered Pepe as he sang; only his own voice, made enormous by the microphone, came booming to his ears. It frightened Pepe and he stopped. "Alberto!" he called suddenly.

But Alberto was nowhere to be seen. He had disappeared.

"That will do, friend," said the Mayor. "We thank you. And now, my friends—" he began.

But the crowd shouted, "Long live the coquis! We want the coqui!" over and over. The Mayor waved his arms up and down and finally they were quiet. He looked at his watch. "We have only a few moments left in which to present the Key-to-the-City to—" he turned to the man beside him—"what *is* the name of that poet fellow?"

"He's gone," the man answered in a sad voice.

"He's *what*?" roared the Mayor.

"Someone came up and pulled him down into the crowd," the man said, more gloomily than before.

"But what will I do with the Key-to-the-City?" the Mayor cried. These words went into the microphone and all the People heard them.

"Alberto!" Pepe yelled into the microphone. It seemed to him that he heard a small voice, far below, coming from somewhere in the heart of the crowd. It said, "Here I am, Pepe! I am coming!" But the crowd began roaring, "Give it to the coqui!" so loudly that Pepe could hear nothing else.

"And so," said the Mayor, wiping his brow, "in token of our appreciation of your great gift of song, of the honor you have paid us all by coming here today, I wish to present to you—to you, that is, on behalf of the People—the Key-to-the-City-of-New-York! I thank you one and all." The Mayor put the Key down beside Pepe and said to the gloomy man, "Come on, we must hurry. I never thought I'd live to see the day: giving the Key to a cricket!"

The crowd clapped and hurrahed. They were still surprised by Pepe's visit and happy that one of their coquis had been honored. The Mayor and his attendants left the platform, and little by little the People below began to scatter. Pepe shouted to Alberto in the microphone, but a man put his head up from under the table and said, "No use doing that any more now." The man's ears were big and he tried to pull his woolen cap down to cover them, but it wouldn't reach. "The mike's off."

"It is? It seems to be still on—on the table," Pepe said.

"Yes, but it's turned off. See what I mean?"

"No."

"Well, never mind; and I must take the table, too."

"You must?"

"Yep. Can't get this cap on straight, my ears are cold."

"Then I'll wait on the floor below the table for Alberto to come back."

"Wouldn't work out, young fellow. That's the platform you're talking about. Have to take that down, too."

"You do?"

"Yep, that's my work. It was just put up for this celebration. Don't know how I'll do it if I can't warm my ears. Cap won't come down right."

"I think your cap is too little to come down," Pepe told him.

"Is that it? Thought it was mighty odd. Couldn't figure it out. My crew will be here any minute."

"It will?"

"Sure will. Say, that was a fine song you did just now."

"That was the song of the coquis. It's part of the Green Song."

"The Green Song, you call it? Well, and in all this snow, too. Great song. Well, now I must be getting to work. Got cold ears, too. Cap don't seem to want to cover them. You're ready to hop down and along, young fellow, so I'll just get things moving around here."

"Down and along where?"

"Wherever you're going. My, the snow is really coming down, isn't it? Take your Key—here."

Pepe tried to pick up the Key. It was many

times larger than he was.

"Tell you what," said the man, "you hop down and I'll hand it to you."

So Pepe hopped from the table and landed in the soft snow. The man placed the Key carefully beside him. "Well, good luck," he said. "Sure enjoyed your singing. Can't seem to get this cap to set right."

"It's too little for you," Pepe pointed out again.

"Wouldn't be at all surprised if *something* wasn't wrong with it. Won't come down over my ears. Well, take care of yourself."

"I must take care of the *Key*," Pepe explained. "For Alberto."

But the man was holding his hands over his cold ears, trying to warm them, and he could no longer hear.

Pepe began dragging the great Key through the snow.

Part Four

It was very hard for Pepe to get through the snow because a coqui needs all four feet to walk with. Pepe could pull the key only a little way, then he had to hop. He couldn't hop very high because the Key was too heavy. And every time he hopped he sank far down into the soft snow and had to dig himself to the top of it again. He went like that, dragging the Key, hopping, sinking, digging; and so it took him a long, long time to get to the street. It was late in the afternoon when he reached the sidewalk, and he was somewhat weary. He leaned against a lamppost to rest and catch his breath.

There was more noise around Pepe than he had ever heard at one time in his life. It was made by the automobiles, and the horns of the automobiles, and the People driving them. There was only snow and noise. At last, when Pepe had caught his breath, he began looking around. Standing right in front of him was a middle-sized boy. The boy was staring at him with big round

eyes as though he didn't believe what he saw.

"I'm Pepe," the coqui said, hoping to relieve the boy's mind.

The boy pointed his finger at Pepe.

"You're a—why, you're a tree frog! You're Eleutherodactylus portoricensis!"

Pepe was astonished. "How in the world do you know that?"

"Oh, I've studied about you. I've seen pictures of you. I never hoped to see you in *person*, though!" The boy spoke breathlessly.

"Well, in that case, now you see me. Very, very few People know my real name and that's why I seldom use it. Also, it is a very long name. And hard to say, too."

"I don't think so," said the boy. "You just take a good long breath and start off: E-leu-thero-dac-tylus, which means tree frog; and por-to-ri-cen-sis, which means you come from Puerto Rico. Together they mean that you're not like any other tree frog anywhere."

"How smart you are!" Pepe said admiringly. "This is not very well understood by most People. In general, I am called a coqui."

"I never heard that name," said the boy.

"Well, now you have."

"That's so," the boy answered. Then he smiled and breathed more easily. "Say, now, you're right! I think it's a fine name. Listen, may I sit here and talk to you?"

Pepe sighed. "Right now? Couldn't you talk

to me some other time? I'm in kind of a hurry just now."

"Oh, sure," the boy said. "Can I give you a lift somewhere? I'm working now, haven't finished my day yet. I ought to hurry, too. I have to take these dresses up to Union Square." He waved his arm toward the street and Pepe saw a sort of cart, all covered over with canvas.

"Where are the dresses?" he asked.

"They're right there. Under that cover. They're hanging on coat-hangers on my cart."

"They are?"

"I'll take you with me; that is, if you want to go."

"Oh, I want to very much!"

"Well, let me lift you up." The boy put his hands around Pepe carefully. Pepe clutched the Key and held his breath. "Say, what's this?" the boy exclaimed suddenly as he touched the Key. It had sunk into the snow. "Is it a part of *you*?"

"Yes. It has to go, too. It's the Key for Alberto."

"Well, sure. Of course it can go. I'll put it between these humps of the coat-hangers and you can hold on to the seam of the canvas. Will that be all right? Or, I could put you in my pocket."

"You could?" Pepe tried to settle himself comfortably on the canvas.

"I carry lots of things in my pockets," the boy said cheerfully. "Oh, pads and pencils and wire and string and rocks and fishing hooks and—"

"No," said Pepe, firmly. "I find I am very

comfortable where I am."

"That's good. Now if you'll just tell me where you're going, I can take you there."

"I'm going to find Alberto."

"Is Alberto another Eleutherodactylus portoricensis?"

"No. He is a poet."

"Where is he?"

Pepe looked at him in surprise. "I don't know!"

It was the boy's turn to think for a moment before answering. Then he said in his cheerful way, "Well, the thing to do is to start out, isn't it?"

"Oh, yes," Pepe exclaimed. He was glad to find that the boy was so sensible.

"My name is Jack," the boy said. He stood beside Pepe, took hold of the rod above Pepe's head and began pushing the cart along. "We have to stay near the curb, or else the automobiles will get in our way."

"They will?" Big cars rushed by them. Pepe and Jack had to shout to hear each other.

"It's great to know you, Pepe!"

"It is?"

"Why, sure. I could have looked all over the fields outside the city and never found *you*. And here you are, sitting right on the curb at City Hall! It's great!"

"What kind of fields are they?"

"They're mostly clover fields. I go out to them on weekends and on my day off."

"Are the clover fields a part of the world?"

"They sure are. The country part. *I* think the

best part."

"What do you do in them?"

"Well, I walk through them sometimes and look at all the creatures that live there, and other times I just run. Then again I sit down on the bank of one of the creeks there and carefully watch people like you. In summer, of course. Can't go in the winter. In summer they're green fields."

"They must be very fine." Pepe began to feel more cheerful.

"Say, Pepe, how did you get here, all the way from Puerto Rico?"

Pepe began to feel warm. Jack had pulled part of the canvas over his head and the snow did not fall on him any longer. "I came in the airplane. I had a ticket my size and they built me a seat. I am visiting the world."

"That's very interesting. I never studied anyone like you before."

"Are you studying me?"

Jack laughed. "Kind of," he said. "I love to study living things."

They went rolling along at a fast pace. Jack pushed the cart expertly while he talked, stopping it now and then and starting it again. "Why do we stop like that, and then start?" Pepe asked him.

"See that little red light way up there through the snow?"

"Now I do," Pepe said. "Is that red? It looks

like a star!"

"It says *Stop!* and I stop."

"It does?" Pepe couldn't hear it, but he thought that was because all the automobiles made such noise.

"Yes, and I rest when it shines. Like this— see? Now a green one comes on. See it?"

"Yes!" Pepe shouted. "A green star! I never saw a green star in my whole life!"

Jack laughed with joy. "And it says *Go!*" As he said the word Jack pushed the heavy cart forward. They went rumbling along. Pepe held tightly to the seam of the canvas. He was enjoying the ride more and more. He looked up on both sides of the street.

"What are those giant things on both sides of us?"

"Those? Why, they're buildings."

"They've got so many eyes! Are they watching us?"

Jack laughed again. "They're windows, Pepe!"

"They look like thin mountain peaks with eyes."

"Oh, they do, Pepe!"

"I'm glad I came to see the world."

"I am, too, Pepe. Seeing you helps me think of the fields. I like to think of them, and when I do it makes my work light."

"It does?"

"Oh, it does. When I'm grown up I'm going to do other work. I'm going to be a teacher. I will teach about living things. And then in the summer I will travel, like you."

"Will you travel to the Island? It's green, too. It's *always* green."

"Oh, will I! You bet! You just wait! Pepe, you're such a good companion!"

"I am?"

"I wish you would come home and stay with me!"

"I can't do that. I must visit the world."

"That's right. And besides, you don't belong in a heated, stuffy house."

"No," said Pepe firmly, "only in my own house. You will come and see my house, when you travel to the Island. I live in a sugar cane field."

"I never saw a sugar cane field."

"Well, you will. And you will meet Juan and Rafael."

"Who are they?"

"They're People, like you. They work in the sugar cane field."

"What do they do?"

"They are very strong and they have great long knives called machetes. They lift up the machetes and then—*wham!*—they cut through the sugar cane and it falls."

"Do you think they might let me help?"

"Well, they might, if they think you'd be careful."

"Oh, I would, Pepe!"

"I'll tell them you are coming when I go back. You will meet Coco. He's a coqui, too. He's another friend."

"Look, Pepe. Here we are! The time passed so quickly, talking to you. This is Union Square."

"It is?" Pepe leaned forward and stared with all his might. He saw great buildings and lights and more automobiles.

"I must take the dresses up into a building near here."

"Then just put me down here on the street," Pepe told him. "I'll go on and find Alberto."

"I hope you find him soon, Pepe," Jack said. He picked up Pepe and the Key with care and held him tenderly with closed fingers a minute. Then he opened his fingers and he and Pepe looked into each other's eyes. "You take care of yourself, Pepe. I don't like leaving you out in the cold like this, but I know it's better for you than an old hot, steamy house."

"Oh, it is!" Pepe exclaimed.

"I'll think about you every day, Pepe."

"You will? You must grow up quickly and come to the Island."

"It won't be long, Pepe. I'm older than I look."

The automobile horns were sounding louder than before. "Oh! My cart is blocking the way! I must go now." Jack put Pepe down carefully. "Good-by, dear Pepe!"

"Good-by, dear Jack!"

Jack was already pushing his cart away. "I'll see you later, Jack!"

"You bet!" Jack called cheerfully. He sent back

a laugh through the falling snow to cheer Pepe as they vanished from each other's sight. One minute Jack had been standing there by his cart, then there was a great white curtain of snow with his laugh behind it, and at last there was only the snow. And the noise of the automobiles.

Part Five

*P*epe sighed. He began going along again in his slow way, pushing the Key, hopping, falling deep into the snow, and digging himself out. "Sometimes the world is sad," he murmured to himself. As he said this Pepe sank down deeper into the snow. He glanced up and saw an automobile going right *over the top* of the hole he was in! "I must be in the middle of the street where Jack said the cars got in your way," he thought. He began climbing out of the hole very fast and managed to get on top of a little hill. It was made of hard snow and ice.

"Oh," thought Pepe, "if those cars got too much in a person's way they could mash a person *flat*!"

Just then there was a louder noise than before. It was a screech. A great automobile headlight shone on Pepe and other screeches sounded. "Hey!" a man shouted angrily, "get out of the way!"

"You're blocking traffic!" another voice yelled.

"I am?" Pepe asked. "I am doing *what* did you say?"

There were more screeches of brakes and

stronger lights. More automobile horns blared around Pepe. A policeman ran over and looked all around. "On the ground!" a man shouted to the policeman. "It's a frog!"

"Where?" the policeman asked, running round in a circle.

"There's a frog right in front of you!" another man shouted, blaring his horn.

"There is?" Pepe asked. Just at that moment Pepe felt it in his bones that it was time to start the Green Work. Keeping one foot on the Key beside him, he raised his voice in song. "Coqui, coqui," he sang. But the moment he opened his mouth the horns began screeching and croaking and the People yelled louder and louder. Pepe knew he was singing, but he couldn't hear a sound he made. "Oh," he thought, "what shall I do? How can I get the notes up to the stars if I can't hear them myself?" He tried to sing louder.

"Hey, you!" the policeman shouted at him.

"Coqui, coqui," sang Pepe.

"Move along! You're blocking traffic!"

Pepe sang on, of course, but even though he knew he was singing he heard no notes. He heard only the screeches and horns. Then there was a new sound. It began low and far away, but the nearer it got the louder it sounded. "Okay, okay," the policeman told the People in the cars all around him. "I'm getting some help. That's the siren."

The siren car came right up to Pepe. "Ooooooooooh," it wailed. And then it stopped,

just when it was loudest. That made Pepe shiver, but he sang on.

Then there were many policemen around. "What's the matter, Mac?" they asked.

"Matter enough!" Mac told them. "There's a frog here that refuses to move along. Rush hour, too!"

"Oh, he refuses, does he?" one of the policemen yelled.

"Causing a jam! Hey, you!"

In all the noise and confusion, Pepe still tried to sing. He was doing the Green Work, but he didn't feel right at all inside. It was the first time in his life that he couldn't hear anyone sing, not even *himself*. Everything was wrong. Pepe began to hurt inside.

"That's enough, boys," said Mac. "I'll take care of him."

"Run him in, Mac!"

"You're under arrest," Mac told Pepe.

"Coqui, coqui," Pepe couldn't talk and try to sing at the same time. "Perhaps Mac doesn't realize that," he thought.

Mac scooped Pepe and the Key up in his hands. "I'll take him in, boys. You straighten out the jam."

Mac put Pepe on the siren car seat and, steering in and out among the cars, he managed to get away from the traffic jam. Then he took off his cap and let out his breath in a long "Whew!"

56

Pepe was still chanting the Green Song. He could hear snatches of it now and then, but it was not going right. That made him have a strange ache inside. Pepe had never felt so sick in all his life.

"Well, that was a fine thing to do, I must say," Mac growled. "Holding up traffic like that in the rush hour. Who do you think you are?"

"Coqui, coqui," Pepe sang feebly.

"How's that again?"

"Coqui, coqui," Pepe sang faintly.

"You sound sort of weak. Anything wrong?"

Pepe nodded "Yes" as hard as he could and kept on, of course, with the Green Work.

"Where does it hurt?" Mac growled again but in a kinder voice.

The ache was somewhere in the middle of himself, so Pepe pointed to his stomach. "Coqui, coqui," he chirped.

"You felt sick, right there in Union Square?"

Pepe nodded his head up and down as strongly as he could. "Coqui, coqui," was all he could say.

"A hick, most likely," Mac said, as if talking to himself. "Got into the middle of the street there and the lights blinded him." He looked down at Pepe. "You look miserable to me. I'm going to get some help for you."

Pepe wanted very much to tell him to try and find Alberto, but it wasn't possible to stop the Green Song just then, weak and puny though it was as it hopped from his throat.

Mac turned the car around. "I'm taking you to a specialist," he said. He drove the car along rapidly.

Like any sensible coqui, who always wants to know exactly what he's doing and where he is going, Pepe wanted to ask Mac what a specialist was. But instead, naturally, he had to go on with the Green Work.

"Yessireee," said Mac. "A friend of mine will get a frog doctor for you. You *are* a frog, aren't you?"

Pepe shook his head. "Coqui, coqui."

"Never heard a frog sound like that, come to think of it. Say, where do you come from?"

Pepe broke into the Green Song and gasped: "Island!"

In all the noise Mac didn't hear him clearly. "Ireland! Well, think of that! My own grandmother came from there. It's a very green place, isn't it?"

This time Pepe's head went up and down faster than ever.

"So you're an Irish frog!" Mac chuckled.

"Coqui, coqui," sang Pepe wearily, shaking his head. Pepe thought of Alberto as he tried to make the Green Song heard above all the noise of the streets through which they were driving. "Oh, where are you, Alberto?" he thought. "*You* could tell Mac who I am!"

At last Mac stopped the car. "Here we are," he said. He picked up Pepe and noticed the Key for the first time. "What's that you've got?"

Pepe tried to lift the Key to show him, but it was too heavy and he was too weak.

"Let me lift it. Why, it's the Key-to-the-City! How did you come by that?"

"How can I tell him?" Pepe thought, so he just continued to sing.

Mac threw back his head and laughed. "Straight from Ireland and he already has the Key-to-the-City! Come along!"

Pepe held on with all his strength to Alberto's Key as Mac carried him through the snow to a great dark building. Mac knocked on the door, but nobody answered. Then he pounded on the door, making the air around Pepe shake with noise. "Open up!" he called.

At last the door opened a little way. Standing in the doorway, with the light behind him, was an old man, tall and very thin, with a long waving mustache.

"Here he is," Mac told Pepe. "O'Brien himself. The watchman."

"Oh, it's you, is it, Mac?" the watchman said.

"I've got a friend with me," Mac answered.

"Coqui, coqui," sang Pepe.

"Got a cold, Mac?" the watchman asked. "You talk, and then you croak—"

"That's not me," Mac laughed. "That's my friend."

"Well, how do you do?" O'Brien asked, holding out his hand. "Come in, come in."

Suddenly the street noises were shut out.

They were in a warm room. Pepe looked at the strong light and blinked. "Coqui, coqui," he sang weakly. No other coqui answered him here, either.

"Well, where's your friend?"

"Right here," said Mac.

The old watchman peered down at Pepe. He smiled. "Another stray, Mac? You're always picking up stray creatures—"

"This one caused a traffic jam a little while ago, but he's no stray. He's an important frog. He's got the Key-to-the-City!"

"He's mighty little to have that."

"And he's from Ireland!"

Pepe tried hard to correct Mac. He tried to say "Island of Puerto Rico" but he was much too weak by now to interfere at all with the Green Song, and it came out, "Coqui, coqui."

"Talks funny, doesn't he?" the watchman asked.

"That's just his brogue, man!" Mac said. O'Brien smiled and Mac roared with laughter at his own joke.

The watchman took Pepe and the Key into his hands and held them both carefully. Pepe still chanted "Coqui, coqui," but now it sounded more like hiccoughs. He was exhausted.

"See here, O'Brien," Mac said in a troubled voice, "get some help for him right away. He's a mighty sick frog."

"Coqui, coqui," Pepe sang faintly, and suddenly the Green Song was ended for the evening. Pepe didn't know whether it had finished or not. He was too tired and ached too much inside to wonder about it. Little by little it had faded out.

Mac and O'Brien talked to each other. A doctor came and put a stethoscope to Pepe's heart. The lights were terribly bright in his eyes. "And they don't know what I am!" Pepe thought. "Oh, Alberto, where are you?" He sighed and put his head down and closed his eyes.

He didn't know if the stars were safe, or if a place had been made in the sky for the sun, or whether the moon had been dusted. It made him feel hot and cold at the same time to think about it, and the worst of all was that he was too weak to do more than think about it. And when he thought about it, he ached, deep in his bones.

Then, all at once, he fell asleep.

Part Six

When Pepe opened his eyes again he was lying on a mossy bank. He was warm. His neatly folded overcoat was beside him and the Key next to it. He heard the music that water makes when it runs and leaps over stones. Beams of sunshine played over his head and suddenly Pepe was glad. A place had been made in the sky for the sun to come up in after all, and there it was—somewhere above him—doing its best to warm the morning.

"The first thing," Pepe thought, "is to discover where I am. So I can tell Alberto, when I find him, what happened to me."

Pepe still felt weak but he sat up and looked around. The mossy bank, with grasses and flowers growing on it, went down gently to a little brook. The water in the brook splashed and danced over rocks and around small islands, then curving around a bend, disappeared from view. "Where it comes from and where it goes is a mystery," Pepe sighed as he drank from it and

washed his face. "But while it passes it makes everything sparkle, like rain does to the Island."

All around were plenty of the things that a coqui likes to eat, and after Pepe had a good breakfast he felt strong enough to do a little exploring. He climbed up the bank and found a tall iron fence. He tried to climb the fence but he could not. He tried to go under it, and there was no way he could do it. So Pepe went in the opposite direction. He crossed the brook and went on through the grasses beyond it. And he came to another fence, just like the first one. Going in a third direction Pepe was again stopped by a fence. "I don't like fences all around me," Pepe frowned.

He now went in the fourth direction and was stopped by a fence again. But here, although he couldn't get through it, Pepe could look beyond it. And across from where he was Pepe saw an enormous animal walking back and forth, back and forth, behind its fence.

"I don't like the fences!" Pepe called out.

"Who does?" the animal growled without interrupting its walk.

"I want to go away from them!" Pepe shouted.

"Ha!" the animal replied. "Walk up and down!"

"What for?"

"To keep in shape," he was told.

"I am in shape. I have my own shape," Pepe said, looking down at himself.

"You won't have it long."

"I won't?"

"Not with all these fences sprouting every way you turn. Walk up and down like me."

"Well, why?"

"Because some day you'll get out from between the fences and then you'll be in shape. Your muscles will be strong. Walk! Don't stop. Don't stop for anything but food. And sleep."

Pepe began hopping all along that side of the fence. He hopped to one end, then turned and hopped to the other end. By that time he was rather tired. "It makes me tired!" he cried.

"That's because you're not in shape. You're flabby! Walk, and keep strong."

Pepe hopped mournfully along. "I don't like the fences."

"Don't be discouraged. Don't moan. Be a lion!"

"Be a what?"

"Be a lion. Like me." Suddenly the lion stopped walking. It held its head high and roared. It roared so loudly that Pepe thought it had thunder in its voice, and he was deaf for a second. He kept on hearing the roar even after it had stopped.

"That's a lion for you!" his neighbor said, and began walking up and down again.

Pepe sat there trembling from the sudden noise and wondering what to do. Soon a man came running up to the lion's cage. "What do you want, Leo?" he cried.

But the lion wouldn't even look at him; he

just walked back and forth. The man shrugged his shoulders and went away.

"That's how I treat *them!*" the lion told Pepe when the man had gone. "Keep them guessing."

"Maybe he wanted to talk to you," Pepe said in a rather small voice.

"What if he did? What do you suppose he's got to say that could possibly interest a lion? I roar, and he comes running!"

"I don't like fences," Pepe told himself. But the lion heard him.

"Hold up your head! Walk up and down! Roar when you feel like it!"

"How can I roar?"

"Throw back your head! Let it out! Have the heart of a lion!"

Pepe threw back his head and tried to roar. "Coqui, coqui," was all he said. "I have the heart of a coqui," he sighed.

"Never get tired, coqui! Never stop!"

"You may call me Pepe."

"What for?"

"Because that's my name," Pepe said.

"Mine's Leo," the lion growled.

"I came to visit the world, Leo, and I never saw a lion before."

"Got thousands of them in Africa," Leo said, going back and forth.

"Is Africa one of the new words?"

Leo stopped in his tracks. He opened his mouth so wide that Pepe thought he was going to roar again. Pepe trembled.

"New word! Africa!" Leo shouted. Then he began walking again the next instant. "Africa is as old as the world. Africa is my home. Africa is the country of lions. Africa is where lions are born and raised."

"Well," said Pepe, "I came to learn about the world, and now I'm learning."

"Walk up and down! Learn about Africa! Don't just *sit* there!"

Pepe hopped back and forth as slowly as he could. "I get tired rather easily, it seems," he told Leo.

"Keep strong! Keep a stout heart! Think of Africa!"

Pepe tried to keep going. He tried to think of Africa but he didn't know what to think about it.

"That's it!" Leo called out encouragingly. "You'll be strong when the time comes to go!"

But Pepe had to sit down. "I'm thirsty," he said.

"Then roar! They'll bring you a drink."

"I can't roar."

"Could if you tried!"

"I tried, Leo."

"Ha! Not hard enough!"

"Besides, I've got water here."

"Well, drink it! Don't talk about it!"

Pepe dragged himself from the fence to the brook. He was panting. He had a drink and then he decided to take a bath. He got into the water and splashed around, but it only made him more weary. He crawled up the mossy bank and fell down. "I think I will have a nap," he told himself. He put his head down on a pillow of moss and was fast asleep in a few moments.

When he woke up he saw a little girl standing in front of his fence, looking at him. "Hello," she said.

"Hello," said Pepe. They stared at each other.

"I'm with the Group," she said.

"You are? What's that?"

"It's Mrs. Kroggs' Play Group. We meet after school and come to play at the Zoo."

"You do? What's a Zoo?"

The little girl stared at him for a few seconds. "Why, it's here—where they keep the animals. Where you are."

"I'm not an animal. I'm Pepe."

"How do you do," she said politely. "I'm Jane."

"That's Leo over there behind you."

"I know. We visit now and then, but he doesn't talk. He seems to have something on his mind."

"He's got Africa on his mind."

"Something like that. He's busy all the time."

"He's keeping strong so he'll be in good shape when he leaves."

"That's sensible."

"I suppose so," Pepe sighed. "But it wears me out. Hopping, hopping, hopping up and down and going nowhere. I'd rather sit and talk."

"Oh, so would I!" Jane agreed.

"You would?"

"Oh, yes. Mrs. Kroggs says I talk too much."

"I love to talk. I came from the Island of Puerto Rico. I rode in a plane. They built me a seat almost an inch big. That's my size."

"I have a friend who rode in a plane. She comes from the Island, too. She's not here now, but her name is Consuelo."

"Yes," Pepe sighed. He was beginning to feel happier.

"It's a beautiful name." Jane sighed, too. Then they looked at each other again, and knew they were friends.

A lady came up to them. "Why aren't you with the Group, Jane?" she asked.

"I was talking, Mrs. Kroggs," Jane said with dignity, "to a friend."

"Talking to a frog? Don't be silly, Jane. Frogs don't talk. They croak."

"He's only a *kind* of a frog," Jane said quietly. "He's really just *himself.*"

"Now let's not allow our imagination to run away with us. What do you really think he is—a prince in disguise?"

"That's rather corny, Mrs. Kroggs, if you will excuse me. He's Pepe. He comes from the Island—Consuelo's home."

"How did you learn that?" Mrs. Kroggs asked. "There's no plaque posted about him."

"Consuelo has talked about people like him. And he told me."

Mrs. Kroggs frowned. "Really, Jane, I shall have to speak to your mother again."

"Nothing will come of it," Jane sighed. "She'll just give me more vitamins."

Mrs. Kroggs took her hand. "Come along, dear. It's much too hot in here. We're starting a game and we need the whole Group."

Jane sighed. "What's your last name, Pepe?"

"Coqui," Pepe told her.

"Mine's Perkins," Jane said.

"Come along, Jane," Mrs. Kroggs said nervously.

"If you look out your back window, Pepe, you can talk to the bear," Jane called loudly as Mrs. Kroggs pulled her away.

Pepe felt sad. He and Jane had only begun to talk and he knew they had much to say to each other. There were so many things about the Island that he wanted to tell her. But suddenly a thought came to him and he cheered up. "Consuelo will tell her!"

Then the back window Jane had mentioned came to his mind. He hopped directly across the mossy bank until he came to the fence again. He walked along it until he found a small window with screening over it. He looked through it and saw a great creature sitting in a cage on the outside of the building where he was. It sat on its haunches and stared off into space.

"You're white!" Pepe called out.

"Polar bears generally are," it answered in a soft, furry voice.

"It's the color of shivering and shaking," Pepe told the bear.

"I beg your pardon?"

"White is. It's snow. It's cold," Pepe explained.

"Ah!" the bear murmured. "That's what *you* say."

"We never have snow where I come from."

"I suppose not," the bear said gently.

"It's green there."

"How unfortunate for you."

Pepe was astonished. "What do you mean?" he asked.

"No snow. No ice."

"It's *always* warm," Pepe said contentedly.

"How gloomy! I could never bear it."

"And I," answered Pepe, "do not care for the snow. Brrr."

"I see you don't wear a fur coat," the bear said.

"No."

"Makes *all* the difference." The bear smoothed its fur delicately with a huge paw.

"Jane told me you were here."

"Oh, I'm devoted to Jane. We have lovely talks. Are you a friend of hers?"

"Yes. I like her, too."

"My name is Nanook."

"Mine is Pepe. I am a coqui."

Nanook looked at Pepe carefully. "There aren't many of you, I suppose?"

"Hundreds and thousands of me! Why do you suppose that?"

"Because I never saw one of your number before."

"And I never saw anyone like you."

"But *that* is absurd. Everyone knows there are thousands of polar bears in Alaska."

"Is Alaska like Africa?"

"Now that," said Nanook, looking at Pepe sharply, "is the oddest remark I ever heard."

"It is?"

"Most certainly."

"Why?"

"Because everyone knows there is no place that can be compared to Alaska."

"Why," Pepe exclaimed, "then it's just like the Island!"

"What's that?"

"My country. Where I came from."

"Even it, dear Pepe," said Nanook softly, "cannot compare. Listen carefully. Try to imagine fields and fields of snow, glistening in the moonlight. Small round houses of ice here and there. Long, long dark nights. Little bears tumbling around. Does that sound like your Island?"

"Not at all!"

"There! You see? It cannot compare."

"But—" began Pepe.

"It is better not to try to compare," the gentle bear said. "Tell me, do you like your quarters here?"

"I do not like the fences," Pepe frowned.

"Oh, don't think about them. Is the rest of

your place comfortable? Is it homey?"

"Not with fences around it."

"Try to take your mind off of those."

"But they're everywhere! How can I do that?"

"Look far off. Look *beyond* them."

"But I can't do that. They are bigger than I am."

"Then look wherever there are no fences. Look up. And dream. Above all—dream."

"Well, I do that at night."

"Do it at other times, too."

"Why?"

"Then you will see far-off places. And only beautiful pure things like snow."

"Brrrr," said Pepe, shivering.

"And little ice houses. And lovely, lovely seals."

"What are they?"

"Seals? They are dear little creatures that go flap, flap, flap over the ice."

"How do they do that?"

"With their flippers."

"They flap with their flippers? How strange the world is!"

"They swim and get nice and fat. Then they go flap, flap, flap over the ice. Ummmmm," said Nanook, looking off into the distance as though seals were there.

"They sound a little noisy."

"Only when they bark. They make no noise when they flap, only a faint squish. They are delicious." The bear stroked its fur carefully.

"Do they have fences in Alaska?"

"Oh, my dear Pepe. That tiresome subject again? You must really raise your thoughts to a nobler level."

"But my eyes are just level with the fences."

"Do you imagine there is nothing finer than what you see? Dreams, and only dreams are the beautiful things in life."

"What a strange way to think!"

"That's why I'm preparing to go to sleep."

"You are? It's not time yet, is it?"

Nanook sniffed the air. "Oh, yes. Winter is here at last."

"Winter? I mean, it's not night. I know it's not because I sing at night."

"Isn't that rather rowdy of you?"

"It is not. I do the Green Work then."

"You needn't bother to explain it to me. It sounds tiresome, if you'll forgive my saying so."

"It isn't. It rests me."

"But it sounds so *active*! Now what you really want to do, Pepe, is to go for a nice long nap."

"I had one a while ago."

"But a *long* one. It's so very pleasant. You will dream and dream."

"I dreamed about the fences."

"Really, Pepe. I must ask you not to tangle up our conversation with unpleasant things."

"Everywhere I hop, I bump into one of them!"

"That's just what you must not do. Don't hop. Dig yourself a deep, deep cave and crawl into it."

"Then what would I do?"

"Why, go to sleep. And sleep for days and days and moons and moons."

"If I did that there would be no moons and moons."

"Why do you say that?"

"Because the Green Work dusts off the moon and helps it to rise, among other things," Pepe said proudly.

"Oh, dear. You bring up *work* again."

"And what would I live on all that time? What would I eat?"

"Ah!" Nanook said softly, "you would live on your fat."

"My fat?"

"Oh, yes. If you stopped all that hopping and tearing around and tiresome working, you would build up a thick coat of fat. And then when you went to sleep you could dream, and live on your fat."

Pepe shook his head. "I feel it wouldn't work with me."

"That *word* again! It would if you tried hard enough. You could improve yourself if you really tried."

"I could?"

"Yes. And now, dear Pepe," Nanook said, sniffing the air, "the time is just right for me to go into my cave and have my lovely dreams."

"Well. Good-by, Nanook."

"Good night, Pepe. A long, long night it will

be, I hope." Nanook spoke softer than ever, then turned and padded silently away.

Pepe went back to the mossy bank and sat down. He saw Leo across the way. He sighed heavily.

"Should I walk up and down or should I dig a cave and crawl into it?" he asked himself. "I think I will dig a cave."

It took a long while, but at last he had a cave in the mossy bank just big enough to fit him. He backed into it carefully and sat, looking out. Everywhere he looked he saw the fences. So Pepe closed his eyes. But even then, with his eyes shut as tightly as he could close them, Pepe still saw the fences all around him. He frowned. But still, wherever he looked, they were there. "I feel like roaring!" he cried. "I feel like Leo does."

He crawled out of the cave and began walking up and down. "That's it!" Leo called to him. "Keep it up! Be a lion!"

Suddenly Pepe stopped walking. He put his foot down. "I am not a lion. I am not a bear. I, Leo," he raised his voice proudly, "am a coqui."

And just at that moment the Green Song began. "Coqui, coqui," Pepe sang, and smiled. He was telling Leo what he was and working at the same time. He could tell that Leo was looking at him, and talking, but he couldn't hear what he said because he had to think steadily of the Green Work and that took all his attention.

But there was no answer to the Green Song.

No other coqui joined in. When Pepe stopped at the places where he was supposed to, there was only silence. The great chorus of coquis, that lifted and raised the song when single coquis rested, was not there. So when Pepe rested, there was a hole in the Green Song. He sang "Coqui, coqui," for quite a while; then when he stopped, there was the hole. That was wrong, Pepe knew. The silence and the hole in the song hurt Pepe inside, but he kept on singing nevertheless, because the Green Song has to be sung.

A coqui cannot wait until everything is right to sing the Green Song. It must be sung on time. "If it is not the perfect song," Pepe sighed, "it is still the best that I can do. It is all that is in me." And he sang on and on. Darkness came and he saw that Leo was no longer walking up and down. Still Pepe sang. He sang as loudly and clearly as he could, but it was not at all his best because the hole in the song hurt him so.

After many hours the song was over. Pepe hopped down to the brook and washed. He felt very weak, and in a little while he sank down on the moss. Soon he was fast asleep.

Part Seven

The next morning the sun came up and shone through open places above Pepe's head. "There it is again," he said. "The Green Song last night couldn't have been as bad as I thought it was."

A small bird hovered outside Pepe's back fence. He noticed it just after he finished his breakfast. The bird fluttered near and then perched on one of the fence bars. It put its head on one side and looked at Pepe out of one of its eyes. Then it turned its head and looked at him out of the other eye. "I don't think it can see straight ahead," Pepe thought.

"Are you sure you aren't a bird?" it asked after a while.

"I'm a coqui. Pepe Coqui."

"But you sing," the bird said. "I heard you singing last night."

"You did?" Pepe was pleased.

"Sure did. I heard you before I went to sleep and every time I woke up I heard you. I said to myself, 'That's a new song!'"

"No. That's a very old song. That is the Green Song."

"I like it. I like that kind of singing. I am a conductor of singing, so I said to myself, 'The first thing in the morning, you go right over and meet that bird.' But you aren't a bird."

"No."

"I thought you might like to sing with our chorus. We give popular concerts at almost any hour of the day. My name is Cyril."

"I sing only in the evening."

Several long, low whistles sounded from far away. "That's my chorus calling me. I must go now."

"Good-by, Cyril."

"Oh, I'll come back later, Pepe," Cyril said as he flew away.

Across the way Leo was pacing up and down. Before Pepe could call out to say good morning, he heard a voice whispering, "Your name, please?"

Pepe looked around but there was nobody to be seen. "Somebody asked my name," he said.

"I did," the voice whispered again.

"You did? Where are you?" Pepe looked in all directions.

"Down here. Inside the cave."

Pepe hopped to the cave he had dug the night before and looked in. Inside was a small gray field mouse. It had a notebook and pencil. "If you will just give me your name, please."

"My name is Pepe Coqui. Why do you hide in the cave and whisper?"

"Sh!" The mouse wrote busily. "We must be very quiet. They don't want people like me in the Zoo. Only rare types like you and the rest."

"I'm not a rare type."

"Didn't they capture you?"

"Nobody captured me. I just went to sleep and when I woke up, I was here."

"Don't speak so loudly. Whisper. If one of the keepers found me here, it would break the chain."

"Where's the chain?"

"The chain of news. Animals like me, who aren't rare, carry news out of the Zoo, and squirrels and chipmunks and starlings and rabbits and sparrows and so on take it to the friends and relatives of the animals here. And we bring back news for them. Now, we need to know more about you. Where do you come from?"

"The Island of Puerto Rico."

"Oh, it will be easy to get word about your friends."

"It will?"

"Oh, yes. There are many ships and planes that go there every day, you know. And birds fly down very often. I will give whatever message you wish to send to a certain friend of mine, a mouse, who goes down regularly by ship. He will get in touch with friends when he lands. He knows a mongoose very well there and he will bring back news to you before you know it."

"How very kind!"

"It's not so much kindness; we all need to

keep in touch with one another, you know."

"Yes," Pepe agreed. "I did not know that up until now when I came to visit the world. But now I know it."

"Why, just the other day we had good news for the jaguar over in the lion house. You can't see him from here; he has the cage behind Leo. Well, we got word from Mexico, where he comes from, that his cousin had had two new babies, twins. His brother had married, and his uncle had discovered a great new water hole for the family. Wasn't that good?"

"Oh, yes," Pepe told the mouse.

"You can imagine how it cheered him. Leo told him about your being here, and he told me. I came over just as soon as I could."

Pepe settled himself comfortably near the mouse. "Tell me your name," he said.

"Rudolph," the mouse answered. "Now I want the names and addresses of your friends or relatives that you need to get in touch with."

"Well, it would be best to get in touch with Alberto, I think."

"Where does he live?"

"I don't know."

"Does he live on the Island?"

"He does. But now he's visiting the world, like me. He's somewhere in New York."

"Oh, I see. We ought to be able to find him. Does he look like you?"

"Oh, no. He's very big. He's a man."

Rudolph dropped his notebook. Pepe saw a gray streak going past him, and Rudolph was no longer at his side. "Rudolph!" he called in a loud whisper.

"Over here," came the answer. Pepe ran as fast as he could and, after looking around here and there, he discovered Rudolph crouching behind a gray rock. He was trembling.

"What's the matter, Rudolph?"

"Oh, what a fright that was!"

"What frightened you?"

"Oh, Pepe. The very idea. Getting news to a *man*. Even the thought makes me tremble."

"Don't tremble, Rudolph. Alberto isn't like most men at all. Look here—" Pepe leaped over a stone and got his overcoat. "He gave me this to warm me, when I was cold in the snow."

"He did? A *man* did?" Rudolph stared at Pepe and touched the coat.

"Alberto," Pepe told him, "is a poet." He folded the coat and put it away again.

"Oh, this is news to carry all over the world! A big man that does not harm little creatures! A poet, you call him? Where is my notebook?"

"It's in the cave. I'll get it." Pepe hopped to the cave, but when he reached down to pick up the notebook Rudolph was there beside him. "How fast you run!" Pepe said.

"I have to be quick. The news I carry can never be told soon enough. And there are so many dangers for a mouse carrying news. Now let me see—" Rudolph wrote in his notebook: "Alberto. No one must fear him. A poet. For Pepe."

Just then Leo roared. "Now that," said Pepe, "makes *me* tremble."

Rudolph looked up from his writing. "Oh, poor Leo. He's not very happy these days and that makes him roar more often. We haven't had any word for him for a long while. That reminds me: there's a ship due in from Africa today. I must run down to the wharves and see if anyone on board—mice, you know—has any news for him." Rudolph put his notebook and pencil in his pocket.

"Farewell for now, Pepe. Try to keep cheered up. I'll let you know the very first minute we have news for you."

Pepe started to say good-by, but by the time he opened his mouth Rudolph was gone.

Leo, with drooping head, was walking up and down. "How do you feel this morning?" Pepe called to him.

"I'm keeping in shape. Why aren't you walking back and forth?"

"Because that is not my way, Leo. It does me no good at all."

"Excuses! Don't let yourself down like that! Never let yourself down!"

Suddenly there was a whirr of wings. Cyril flew past the back window. He swooped around and glided back. Pepe ran over. Just in front of Pepe Cyril halted, fluttering in the air. He pointed with one stretched wing. "He's here!" he cried.

"Who is here?" asked Pepe. But he asked the empty air. Cyril had flown off.

Then a flock of birds whirred past. They circled and when they sailed back they began singing a gay song. They whistled and chirruped, beating time in the air with their wings. Then they, too, flew away.

"Oh," sighed Pepe, "if only I could be outside these fences like they are!"

He heard someone breathing heavily behind him. He turned and saw Rudolph standing there. "I have news," he panted.

"I thought you went to the wharves, Rudolph."

"I started. But when I went by the reindeer's cage they told me there was a *man* going all over the Zoo asking for you."

Pepe was astonished. "Why, it's Alberto!" he cried joyfully.

"That's what I thought," Rudolph tried to catch his breath. "I told Cyril to tell you. And I ran faster than I ever ran before."

"Where is he now?"

"Over near the kangaroos. Cyril is leading his chorus in a big flight. They will try to catch his attention and bring him here."

"You must wait and meet him!"

"Oh, thank you very much. I would like to," the little mouse was nervous. "I don't expect you will understand, Pepe, but I—just couldn't." And

Rudolph disappeared.

Outside his back window Pepe saw the chorus of birds swooping through the air, this way and that. They were singing merrily. Cyril whirred by, whistling, "He's coming, he's coming, he's coming!"

Suddenly Pepe heard a shout. Standing between Pepe's window and the polar bear's cage, with birds flying all around him, was Alberto!

"I've found you, Pepe! Oh, I've found you!"

"Alberto! Here I am!"

Alberto ran up to the window. "How have you been, Pepe? The crowd caught me up that day and I couldn't get back to you!"

"I knew something like that happened," Pepe said.

"But you don't look well, Pepe."

"Well, Alberto, there is a hole in the Green Song. It hurts me."

"We must take care of that right away. I will go now and find the manager of the Zoo. Then I will come back."

With Cyril flying in front, the birds whirled away after Alberto.

Pepe went down to the brook for the last time and drank some water. Then he hopped to the front window. "I am going now, Leo!" he cried.

"Good luck!" Leo growled as he walked back and forth.

"I will think about you after I'm gone."

"When you think about me—roar!"

"Leo, everybody can't roar."

"They don't try. Let it out! Roar when you feel like it!"

"Well, good-by, Leo."

Suddenly Leo sat down and opened his mouth wide. His roaring shook the air. When it was over, Leo cocked his head on one side and winked at Pepe. "That's the way to say good-by, Pepe. Don't feel sad. Some day I will go, too."

"Yes," Pepe answered in a small voice.

There was a fluttering of wings at the back fence. Cyril was outside the window, dancing in the air. "They're coming!" he sang.

Alberto and a strange man walked up to the fence. The man turned a key in a lock and the whole back fence opened. "Oh!" cried Pepe, as he looked through the big opening and saw the bright blue air beyond. His heart beat fast.

"You are free, free, free!" Cyril chanted. The chorus of birds swooped up and down in the air, circling always around Alberto. Alberto laughed and reached inside Pepe's cage. He put Pepe's overcoat on him and fastened it with a safety pin. Then he lifted him up.

"Here is your Key," Pepe said.

"It is your Key, Pepe. But I'll keep it for you if you like." Then he lifted Pepe up on his shoulder.

When Pepe came out of the heated cage he shivered. Cyril flew by and touched him with a wing.

"How does it feel, Pepe? How does the blue air feel?"

"Cold," Pepe told him. "This is Alberto, Cyril."

"Hi, Al," sang Cyril.

"Hello, Cyril."

"You and Pepe must come home with us and celebrate."

"Thank you. Where do you live?"

"Nearby. Come along, and we'll show you." Cyril and the birds flew ahead, with Pepe and Alberto following.

"I read in the paper that a policeman found somebody your size who had the Key-to-the-City, and took him to the Zoo," Alberto said as they walked along. "I knew that was you, Pepe."

"It was in the paper?"

"Very often they write a story in the paper about the Zoo, and today it was about you. I hurried over, but no one seemed to know where you were. I looked everywhere. And then I saw the birds. They flew around my head and I thought, 'Maybe they are friends of Pepe's,' and I followed them."

It was warm near Alberto's collar as they strolled through the snow. "Rudolph, who is a mouse, told them to bring you to me. He was going to find you for me."

"He would have, I'm sure."

"Only you found me first. He's a little frightened of you. You are a man."

"Yes, I know," Alberto said. "And a mouse is a mouse."

"Rudolph is a very brave mouse," Pepe told him. "He's just shy."

By now they had walked far into a grove of trees. Just ahead they saw Cyril and all the birds on a bench. They were brushing off the snow with their wings, sweeping it in all directions. There was so much snow flying about when Alberto and Pepe came up to the bench that it seemed to be snowing again. Soon the bench was dry and clean. "Welcome to our home," said Cyril. "Have a seat."

"We are happy to be here," Alberto told all the birds. Then he sat down. Pepe hopped down and sat on the bench.

"I like your home, Cyril," said Pepe.

"It's not so big as some, of course," Cyril said modestly, "but it will do. We call it Central Park. It has quite a nice view."

A little bird came up to Pepe. "Have some snow," it said, holding out its wing on which there was a pinch of snow.

"Thank you," Pepe said. "What will I do with it?"

"Hold it in your mouth, and it will melt. Then you drink it."

Pepe did as he was told while the bird watched. "It tastes very fine," he said.

The bird sang happily as it fluttered into the air. "It is maple snow."

"She means it came from a maple tree," Cyril explained.

"I prefer oak snow," said another bird flying close to Alberto. "Try it." He held out a wingful of snow.

"It's very good," Alberto said.

Many birds who had been watching them carefully, fluttered into the air. "They like maple and oak snow," they told each other.

"And now for the feast!" cried Cyril, diving upward. "Come on!" The chorus followed with a rush of wings. There was a loud humming and a burst of song. Then the birds flew away.

"They've gone," said Pepe.

"They went to have the feast, I suppose," said Alberto.

It was very quiet in the park. Alberto took out his watch and looked at it. "I must be at the airport very soon to take a plane back to the Island. I was going back earlier but I had to find you first, Pepe. You will come back with me?"

"There is something in my mind that tells me I have not seen the world entirely."

"No one can do that," Alberto answered gently. "And you are not well."

"But there is something I must see. Something that Juan and Rafael told me to see."

"Look up! look up!" sang Cyril's voice overhead. Pepe and Alberto looked up and saw all the birds flying in a circle above. Slowly they came closer and closer until they were just over

the bench. "Hold out your hands!" cried Cyril.

Pepe and Alberto held out their hands. "I wonder what it means," said Pepe.

The birds opened their beaks and a rain of little hard things fell on Pepe and Alberto.

"Dried seeds!" Cyril called out.

"Acorns!" another bird sang.

Alberto gathered up the seeds and acorns as they fell. They were scattered everywhere and more kept falling. "Do you like the feast?" Cyril asked, flying by.

"Oh, yes," Alberto replied, chewing on an acorn.

"It's a little dry," said Pepe.

"Have some snow." A small bird perched on Alberto's arm and offered snow from its wings. "It's maple."

Pepe tried to chew a dried seed. "It's a very fine feast," he said to all the birds.

The birds stayed in the air, flying far away and returning with more seeds and acorns. "Oh, you give us more than we need," Alberto laughed.

"Of course," Cyril sang. "That's what a feast is for!"

Alberto looked at Pepe. "In that way it's just like a feast at home, isn't it?" he asked. Pepe nodded; he was having quite a difficult time eating birds' food.

A bird settled near Pepe. "I'm so glad you're free," it said. Before Pepe could answer, the bird looked at him lovingly, dropped a tiny, speckled worm beside him and flew away.

The speckled worm wiggled itself upright and stared at Pepe. "I was just sitting there," it said indignantly, "minding my *own* business when this creature *swooped* down out of nowhere and *dragged* me from my doorstep, straight into the *air*—"

"Quick, run!" Pepe told it, putting it on the bench.

It humped its back. "I've never been so *mortified* in my life!" it said as it hurried out of sight. Pepe sighed in relief to find that no one but Alberto had noticed the speckled worm.

Cyril handed him a dried leaf. "Have a napkin," he said.

"It was a fine feast," Pepe said politely.

"And now," Cyril sang out, "everybody gather round."

The whole chorus came to hear, perching on the bench and on small bushes nearby, all fluttering and chattering. Cyril raised himself on tiptoes and shouted "Speech! Speech!" to Pepe.

"Speech!" the birds echoed.

Pepe stood up. "Dear and kind friends," he began.

The birds in the bushes arranged their feathers and changed seats with each other. "He called us 'dear'," they told each other. "He said 'kind friends'," they whispered.

"Quiet!" Cyril trilled out the sound in a long, warning note. The birds tried hard to be still.

"Kind friends, I want to thank you for helping

me to go away from the fences. And I want to ask you to thank Rudolph for me, too. I like the world. Sometimes it is cold and sometimes it is warm—"

A small bird, bursting with song, sprang from her seat and soared above them. "It is warm, warm, warm!" she caroled.

"Sh!" Cyril flew after her. She sank immediately back into her seat. She ruffled her feathers. "Please pardon her, Pepe. She thought you meant that spring was coming when you said it was warm. It is her duty to announce spring the moment she hears it is here."

"Oh, that's all right," said Pepe.

"It is difficult for birds to sit still," Cyril explained.

"Oh, I like them to fly about. It makes me feel free, too," Pepe told him.

When the birds heard these words they rose at once into the air, making it lively with the trills and runs which they sang.

"They are like little flutes," Alberto said.

"Well," Cyril sighed. "That was a fine speech, Pepe."

"A speech should not be too long," Pepe murmured.

"It was the right length for Pepe's speech," Alberto said. "He is not feeling too strong."

"Oh, Pepe! I'm sorry!"

"Well, Cyril, there is a hole in the Green Song."

"That's awful! How can you bear it?"

"It's not good for him to be away from home too long," Alberto told Cyril.

"Oh, I know!" Cyril said. "We must leave our home today."

Pepe was surprised. "You must?"

"Yes. Something happened out in the West, and Rudolph wants us to go and find out about it. It was a very strange thing, and Rudolph wants us to discover if any of the relatives of those in the Zoo were injured. Something fell out of the sky."

Instantly Pepe sat up straight. "*What?*" he asked. "What fell out of the sky?"

"They think it might be a meteor. We will fly in relays; other choruses of birds will join us on the way."

"What is a meteor?" Pepe asked quickly.

"I think that it is a piece of a star."

"Alberto!" Pepe cried. "We must leave at once!"

"But, Pepe, you said there was something you had not seen—"

"It doesn't matter, Alberto. I must go home right away. Before something worse happens!"

"Why?" Cyril asked. All the birds gathered around, fluttering anxiously.

"Well, the hole in the Green Song is not only bad for me," Pepe explained. "When there is a hole in it, there is a hole in the sky, too."

"But, Pepe—" Alberto began.

"The Green Song must be whole to keep

everything together. I will go at once and mend the hole. Then nothing else will fall out. Come on, Alberto."

Alberto lifted him up on his shoulder. "Good-by, Cyril," Pepe said. "Good-by, everyone."

"Come to the Island!" Alberto cried. "We will feast together again!"

"Just a moment," Cyril told them. He called the birds together. This time they sat on a single bush and were perfectly still. Cyril stood before them with his wings held high. "We will sing good-by," he said. He brought his wings down and the chorus began to sing. Instead of wings, melody flew in the air around Pepe and Alberto. Pepe thought he had never heard such a song before.

Alberto looked at him and nodded. "Yes, Pepe," he said. "It lifts the heart."

"Oh, it does!"

"That is the work of birds."

Alberto and Pepe left the park with the birds' song ringing in their ears. "I will never forget it," Pepe whispered. "It is almost as fine as the Green Song."

Part Eight

When they came to the street Alberto called a taxi. They got inside and drove quickly to the airport. "I think we will be on time," Alberto said as he paid the driver. "But we must hurry."

"I must get my ticket," Pepe said.

"Didn't you get a return trip ticket?"

"No. I got a New York ticket. We must run, Alberto. You don't know what a long time they take to make out a coqui ticket."

Alberto ran. They went up to the ticket window, and Pepe hopped down to the counter in front of it. "I would like a ticket to the Island. A coqui ticket. I am almost an inch size. I was measured before and I haven't time to be measured again. You don't need to build me a seat. Alberto will sit me on his shoulder. We are in a hurry." Pepe spoke breathlessly.

"Here you are, sir," the man smiled, handing Pepe a ticket. It was just his size.

Pepe was astonished. "Alberto, he had it all ready!"

"Hurry, Pepe!" Alberto picked him up, and in a very few minutes they were in the plane.

The stewardess stared sharply at Pepe, sitting on Alberto's shoulder. "No pets allowed in the passenger section," she said.

"That is no pet, madam!" Alberto spoke abruptly. "He gives his friendship, or he keeps it. That is a coqui!"

Pepe was pleased. He sat very proudly.

"Oh," said the stewardess. "Is that a coqui? I didn't know. Please excuse me. Right this way, sir."

The stewardess led them forward in the plane. She showed Alberto to a seat, and there beside it, near a window, was a seat that would just fit Pepe.

"Is this the plane we came up on?" Pepe asked Alberto.

"I don't think so."

"How is it that you have a seat my size?" Pepe asked the stewardess, as he sat down.

The stewardess arranged a pillow at Pepe's back. "We have coqui-size seats on all planes between here and the Island now."

"You do? That wasn't the case when I came up to visit the world. They had to make a seat to fit me."

"We heard about that," she said, "and ever since then the company has been waiting for your return. They wanted to be ready, so they wouldn't have to hold a plane like they did before when you sang your—what is it called?"

"My Green Song," Pepe told her contentedly.

"That's it. It seems that many people in the airport became excited then."

"But it's not time for it now. It is sung when the sun goes down, and the sun is overhead, I think. Or nearly so."

"Well, the company just wanted to be sure, you understand, that everything went well when you returned. And the passengers have heard about you. They ask, 'Where is the coqui seat?' the minute they get on the plane. They seem to like it. Many people call you the Pioneer Coqui, and I wouldn't be surprised if the company left the small seats, just to avoid any, well—excitement—if more coquis decided to travel in the future. Your ticket, sir?"

"Here. It is just—"

"Just your size. We know about *that*, too. Thank you, sir." And after taking Alberto's ticket the stewardess left.

"Well," said Alberto, laughing. "It seems people know who you are, Pepe!"

"It is much better than when they don't know," Pepe answered. "It is more comfortable."

The plane began rising. Alberto leaned over and unpinned Pepe's overcoat.

"I see the tops of the buildings. When I was down in the world I saw the bottoms of the buildings. Look, Alberto! What is that?"

"That is one of the new words, Pepe. It is

called violet. It is the color of New York when it is not snowing."

"Alberto!" Pepe was excited. "I have just remembered! You know there was something I had not seen? Something that Juan and Rafael told me about?"

"Yes?"

"Now I remember! It was the new words in the water!"

"Of course, Pepe! How could I have forgotten! We will look for them when we get over the ocean."

The plane sailed out across the Atlantic. The sun shone and the water sparkled below.

"Alberto, what is that?"

"That's it, Pepe. That's the great water. It's not blue like the sky, is it?"

"It is blue with very much green mixed in it," Pepe smiled.

"And see, Pepe, those specks of white on it?"

"Is that snow?"

"Those are the whitecaps on the waves of the water."

"That was one of the words! Waves!"

"Yes. The water is always moving. We call its movements the waves."

Pepe was astonished. "The waves are like the wind in the air, but you can see them!"

A giant rainbow spread across the heavens. "Alberto!" Pepe cried when he saw it.

"That is a rainbow, Pepe. If you look at it

closely you will see all the new words that Juan and Rafael told you to look for. There they are! Pink and gold and purple and brown and lavender and red and green, too!"

Pepe stared at the rainbow. Then he looked at the blue-green water playing below with its whitecaps. He was very quiet for a long, long time. Then he whispered, "It is like *seeing* the Green Song, Alberto."

Alberto nodded.

Pepe looked at the changing colors all during the afternoon.

"Those colors are in everything," Alberto told him. "After you have seen them like that, separate and bright, you can see them, little by little, in everything. In people and trees and gardens and fields and buildings—in everything!"

Pepe reached over and patted Alberto's hand. "It would be very sad," he said slowly, "if the world were *only* green."

Part Nine

The sun crossed the sky while the plane flew toward Pepe's home. At last there was a change in the song of the motor. "Where are we now, Alberto?" he asked.

"We are there. The Island is below."

Pepe looked down and saw his Island, brilliant as the rainbow from the setting sun. "It is of all colors," Pepe said. "And it is just my size."

"Mine, too," Alberto answered.

The plane came down gently and skimmed along the runway. When it stopped Alberto rose. "You won't need your overcoat here, Pepe."

"It kept me very warm on my visit. I don't know what I should have done without it."

"You must keep it, Pepe. In case you go on another journey." He folded it neatly and lifted Pepe up. "We are home," he said.

"Did you have a nice trip?" the stewardess asked Pepe as they left the plane.

"Oh, yes. I saw the new words in the water and also in the sky."

"They told me you would be seeing things," she remarked.

"And you can see them everywhere if you will look carefully," Pepe told her. "Good-by."

People came running from every part of the airport. They surrounded Alberto.

"Welcome home!" they shouted.

"Thank you," Alberto said. "I cannot tell you how good it is to be here!"

"It said in the paper that the Mayor gave you the Key-to-the-City!" a man cried.

"Not to me! To a coqui!" Alberto said happily.

"Listen to him!" a lady said. "How modest he is!"

"That's just like Alberto!" the man shouted.

"But it is the truth!" Alberto told them all. "See, he is here, too. On my shoulder!"

"Hello," Pepe said to everybody around. He and Alberto had a difficult time getting through the crowd. They had to go slowly through the waiting room while the People shouted and greeted Alberto.

"Welcome! Welcome!" they cried. Alberto waved his hat, and Pepe bowed to them all from his shoulder seat. At last they were out of the airport.

"I will carry you to the sugar cane field, Pepe. You just tell me the direction as we go along."

"It is quite far. Are you sure you want to carry me so far?"

"Of course. I want to see where you live, so I can come to see you often."

"You will? I am so glad, Alberto! You will meet all my friends!"

"And I'll bring my guitar and my friends and I will sing sometimes to *you*. Fair exchange, you know!"

They walked through the warm air, out on the road. It began to get dark as they left the city.

Pepe felt it in his bones that it was time to sing. "Coqui, coqui," he began rather weakly.

From the side of the road another coqui joined in. For a second Pepe was surprised. He kept on singing and other coquis came into the song. Soon more and more were singing. Pepe began feeling better. The notes hopped from his throat and began climbing up into the sky. The song grew and Pepe's own notes became stronger and stronger. They reached very high and began dusting off the stars. They brushed some clouds aside.

"The Green Song is mended!" Alberto shouted.

Pepe's heart was light and happy. The Green Song came pouring into his ears from all sides and began filling the sky. Alberto walked deeper and deeper into the country, hearing the Green Song everywhere. Far in the distance a silver streak showed. Pepe's notes grew rounder and louder and firmer. The Green Song was lifting the moon!

"Soon I will see Juan and Rafael and Coco," Pepe thought. "I will tell them about the world."

By the light of the moon Alberto and Pepe walked on down the road. On both sides grew

flowering trees, making the warm night warmer with their color. "I will be carrying the news like Rudolph, the mouse. I will tell everyone the world is beautiful and whole like the Green Song," thought Pepe, as he held on to Alberto's collar and sang on and on and on.